"A succinct and accessible study of [ ]
making process. This tool lays a solic [ ]
'Jesus journey' and provides a way t [ ]
makers."

—GREG OGDEN, author, *Discipleship Essentials*, chairman,
Global Discipleship Initiative

"What a gem to have this basic training for following Jesus as a companion to
The Discipleship Gospel. The authors have created a great resource that takes
the mystery out of discipleship. Use this step-by-step guide to discover just how
simple it can be to help others grow in Christ."

—JOANNE KRAFT, founder, Grace & Truth Living; author, *The Mean
Mom's Guide to Raising Great Kids*

"Ben and Bill lead you on a journey toward embracing the gospel, growing as
a disciple, and helping others do the same. An interactive and deeply personal
study, this workbook serves as a valuable tool for new believers and a great
refresher for those who have walked with Jesus for many years."

—KEVIN G. HARNEY, Lead Pastor, Shoreline Church; author,
Organic Outreach books

"I've led many groups through this material mostly in an African context,
and it provides an excellent framework for being a follower of Christ, even in
international contexts."

—TIMM SASSER, Director of Development, Empower One

THE
DISCIPLESHIP
GOSPEL
WORKBOOK

MULTIPLY DISCIPLES WITH
THE GOSPEL OF MARK

Ben Sobels & Bill Hull

A Discipleship•org Resource

Dedicated to Cypress Community Church

Dear Reader,

Whether you've believed in Jesus for a short time, for a long time, or never before, this workbook is for you. We've designed it to help you learn Jesus' gospel and how to follow him. It will be especially helpful for those who have never been intentionally discipled by someone. By completing this discipleship experience, you will learn these skills for following Jesus:

How to read and study the Bible
How to start putting Jesus' teachings into practice
How to start living out the foundational practices of discipleship
How to let Jesus change your life by experiencing his gospel for yourself

This workbook leads you through the Gospel of Mark in the Bible, so you'll need your own Bible for individual study. We use the *English Standard Version* throughout this material, but you can use any translation of your choosing. As you complete each lesson, use the answer key in the back of this workbook. Make sure to look there *before* each group meeting, not after. Take at least twenty minutes *before* each session to use that key to fill in the answers as you prepare. Looking at the answers for this workbook ahead of time might seem counterintuitive, but doing so will show your commitment to the group, help you contribute to discussions, and give your group's discussions a solid baseline from which to start.

We suggest you read *The Discipleship Gospel* (to which this workbook is a companion) as you go through this material because it contains vital context to help you understand the content of this workbook. In the Leader's Guide below and at the end of the workbook, we suggest specific chapters of *The Discipleship Gospel* that will take you deeper into the core content of this workbook.

One of the strengths of this discipleship experience is that you get to "count the cost" before you fully commit. Do the first session! See what it's like by trying it out. If you realize it's not for you, you can bow out if you choose, but try the first session before you decide. We think you'll find that Jesus is too intriguing to stop. Jesus is the most important and most beautiful thing that has happened to this world, and we can't wait for you to experience him!

For the advancing of Christ's kingdom,

Ben & Bill

www.thebonhoefferproject.com

WORKBOOK LEADER'S GUIDE

What We Have Learned by Leading Others

1. As a general rule, it's best to have someone lead you through this workbook before you try to lead others through it. If someone else has not led you through it, see if that's possible first. Then, take others through it.

2. Pray hard before inviting people to join your discipleship group (as Jesus did in Luke 6:12-13). Don't just look for people you enjoy the most or with whom you feel the most comfortable. Let God direct you through prayer to the people *he* wants you to disciple.

3. Don't let your discipleship group devolve into a mere *knowledge-based class*; it should be an *obedience-based experience*. It's not about "getting through the workbook" but about learning to live with Jesus and love others like Jesus.

4. When a discipleship group forms, the leader should ask each member to begin praying for two or three people they know who aren't yet following Jesus—that they would begin following Jesus.

5. Encourage your group members to use the "Answer Key" in the back and emphasize with them to use it *before* your group meetings. This might seem counterintuitive, but it will greatly enhance your group's discussions when you all start with "the right answers." Set the tone as the leader by filling out the answers for yourself, even if you know the answers or have been through this material before—speed of the leader, speed of the pack.

6. There are notecards in the back of the workbook to help your group complete the memorization projects. Encourage everyone to use these as they memorize definitions of the gospel, discipleship, and memory verses from the Gospels of Matthew and Luke.

7. Carefully follow the instructions of this workbook by answering each question and doing each project without skipping *this* or *that*. If you skip things, your group experience will decline with increasing measure. This includes reading each chapter out loud as a group. In the first century, disciples would read Scripture aloud, so make that a priority for your group, too.

8. This workbook is most effectively facilitated in gender-specific groups of three or four participants (Tit. 2:1-8), including the leader. It has been used in mixed groups and with other sizes, but in our experience, that's not as effective.

And it's not designed to go through on your own—not at all.

9. Be sure to set a weekly meeting time based on input from those in your group. Once your group sets the time, keep it. As the leader, if you repeatedly miss sessions or change the time, you'll quickly lose momentum.

10. While it may be convenient to meet on your church campus, meetings for this workbook work better in "the public square," so meet at a coffee shop, a restaurant, or another public space. This offers a practical way of making your faith public from the beginning.

11. Important: Once your discipleship group completes Mark 8, ask each person to lead *at least one chapter* (two is even better!) of the studies that cover Mark 9-16. It's not hard to facilitate the group and it gives people much-needed confidence. So, let them lead (under your supervision) and help them if they falter, affirming them with grace, patience, and encouragement.

12. Also important: This discipleship experience isn't finished when your group completes this workbook. That's just the halfway point. It's not complete when we've merely *been discipled*. Full obedience to Christ includes *making disciples*, too (Matt. 28:19-20). That's why we used the term "multiply" in the subtitle of this book. Encourage group members to multiply by leading their own group. If you think members of your group may not be ready to lead their own group, ask them to be an apprentice leader with you in your next group.

13. When your discipleship group meets to read the next chapter of Mark's Gospel, we recommend that your leader start the discussion by asking *one of these four* relational, others-focused questions, which we call "Discipleship Group Starter Questions":

- How have you seen God's goodness this week?
- How are you doing with loving the people God has already put in your life?
- How has God been speaking to you through his Word and prayer?
- Who are two or three people who are not yet following Jesus that you are praying for?

14. You will also find in the back of the workbook a page called "Share Your Jesus Story." Once your discipleship group finishes Mark 16, meet one more time so each member of your group can share their "Jesus Story," along with the gospel, in three to five minutes. Use this time to talk through next steps for multiplying your group.

MARK 1: GOSPEL BEGINNINGS

Mark's Gospel is one of the most helpful, reliable, and historically verifiable sources on the life of Jesus. Read Mark 1:1-45 out loud with your discipleship group. Your leader will help you answer the observation, interpretation, and application questions. If you're not comfortable reading, let your leader know.

OBSERVE: What Do You See?

- Mark 1 serves as the introduction to this Gospel and is filled with activity: Jesus was baptized by John, was tempted by Satan, and began his public ministry. He was about _____ years old at the time (Luke 3:23).

- When Jesus began his public ministry in Mark 1, he began preaching the _____ (Mark 1:14) as his main message. If we are going to truly understand Jesus, we must grasp his _____ .

1. The major declaration of Jesus' gospel in Mark 1:15 was about the kingdom of God. What did Jesus declare about God's kingdom?

2. How did Jesus call people to respond to his declaration about God's kingdom? Read Mark 1:15-17. What were the three aspects of Jesus' call?

-

-

-

3. The Primary Call of Jesus' Gospel: Two of the most powerful words Jesus ever said were "_____ ." These words call us to begin living a new life with Jesus; a life of *seeking first the kingdom of God* (Matt. 6:33).

4. Jesus revealed four of the seven essential elements of his gospel in Mark 1:14-17. With your leader's help, fill in these four gospel elements by the following drawing. (Clue: One goes with the Declarative Statements, three with the Imperative Responses.)

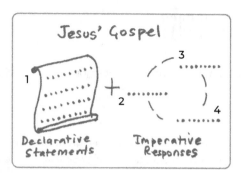

INTERPRET: What does it mean?

5. Read Romans 1:16 and 1 Corinthians 15:1-3. What do these verses teach us about Jesus' gospel? What questions does this study of the gospel raise for you so far?

APPLY: How does it apply?

The "Follow" Project: You've just finished the first session—well done! Now you need to decide whether or not you want to keep learning how to follow Jesus. Take time to decide this week. Count the cost. Maybe you're not ready. When you've made your decision, let your group leader know. If you decide to continue, you're making five commitments:

• I will finish this study of Mark's Gospel with my discipleship group.
• I will make our weekly sessions a high priority on my schedule.
• I will be on time, come prepared, and participate.
• I will transparently share and keep confidential what others share.
• I will multiply this experience by leading a discipleship group myself.

_____

Your Signature

Pray: A.C.T.S. This is a helpful acronym for praying. **Adoration**: Start praying by focusing on God and his goodness. **Confession**: Acknowledge your need for God and confess any sin in your life to him. **Thanksgiving**: Give thanks to God for his forgiveness and for the Holy Spirit who empowers us to obey Jesus. **Supplication**: Pray for others and for various things in your own life.

MARK 2: WHO IS JESUS?

Application Follow-Up: Why did you commit to joining this discipleship group?

Read Mark 2:1-28 out loud with your discipleship group, and your leader will help you answer the observation, interpretation, and application questions.

OBSERVE: What Do You See?

- Take note: Mark 2 is structured around four questions about Jesus (vv. 7, 16, 18, 24). In each case, Jesus' answers led his listeners to consider who he really was—specifically, if he truly was _____ , God's Son.

- Three of the four questions in Mark 2 were asked in the context of eating a meal. Including this event, Mark's Gospel records seven different meals during which Jesus ate with his disciples, and these meals carried with them very important discipleship moments.

Read the four verses below and write out the question asked in each verse on the lines. Then, follow the instructions to learn how Jesus answered them.

1. Mark 2:7: _____ ?
Read Jesus' answer in verses 9-12. (Clue: What did he have the *authority* to do?)

2. Mark 2:16: _____ ?
Read Jesus' answer in verse 17. What did Jesus imply he was able to do? (This is a hard question. Clue: It has to do with declaring sinners righteous.)

3. Mark 2:18: _____ ?
Read Jesus' answer in verses 19-20. How many times did Jesus describe himself

s *the bridegroom*? _____ Read Isaiah 61:10, which is an Old Testament prophecy of the coming Christ. Who did Jesus imply he was?

. Mark 2:24: _____ ?
Read Jesus' answer in verses 25-26. To which Old Testament person does Jesus ken his actions? _____ (1 Sam. 21:1-6). In Jesus' day, one title people used for God's promised Savior was "_____." Like "the oridegroom" referenced earlier, associating himself with King David was a claim to be the Christ, God's Anointed King.

INTERPRET: What does it mean?

. As you think through Jesus' four answers in Mark 2, write a summary of who esus claimed to be and what he claimed to have authority (or power) to do.

APPLY: How does it apply?

The "Dinner with Disciples" Project: Some of Jesus' most poignant moments with his disciples happened around a dinner table. Just as we saw Jesus eat with his disciples in Mark 2, get together as a discipleship group for dinner in our leader's home. If you're married, your spouse is welcome. During dinner, share with each other where you are in your journey with Jesus.

Pray: A.C.T.S. – Adoration, Confession, Thanksgiving, Supplication

MARK 3: DISCIPLE

Application Follow-Up: What did you learn by having dinner together?

Read Mark 3:1-35 out loud with your discipleship group, and your leader will help you answer the observation, interpretation, and application questions.

OBSERVE: What Do You See?

- Mark 3 highlights when Jesus began intentionally discipling a few men. The word "disciple" means *learner.* In ancient times, disciples literally followed their teacher to learn how to live *like him* by living *with him.*

- As you answer the following questions, pay special attention to Mark 3:13-19, which contains a critical moment of Jesus' ministry. He set apart twelve men to disciple them. It is important to note the number he chose, which reveals that discipleship is most effective in small groups.

1. Carefully reread Mark 3:14-15. What was Jesus' first stated purpose for The Twelve disciples, the first thing he wanted them to do (v. 14)?

First:

2. In these verses, Jesus set apart twelve men for three purposes. What are the other two purposes for which Jesus set his disciples apart?

Second:

Third:

INTERPRET: What does it mean?

3. At its core, discipleship is spending time *with Jesus* so we can learn to live *with* him and love others *like* him. Jesus spent 90 percent of his time with
_____ men (Bill Hull, *Conversion and Discipleship*, 145). It's also important to note that he spent more time with just _____ disciples. As we keep reading through Mark's Gospel, we see Peter, James, and John were with Jesus during his greatest highs and lows (1:16-20; 5:37; 9:2; 13:3; 14:33).

4. Read Acts 4:13. What did the religious leaders recognize about Peter and John in this verse that was unique to them as "uneducated, common men"?

Jesus preached to crowds and taught in large groups, but he intentionally trained his disciples in a small group of twelve men with a focus on just three of them. Of all the group sizes, the relational dynamics of his group of three disciples proved to be most transformative.

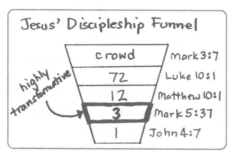

5. In what ways is time with your discipleship group also time with Jesus?

APPLY: How does it apply?

The "Discipleship Definitions" Project: Congratulations! As you study Jesus' teachings and put them into practice with your discipleship group, you're already being discipled and learning how to make disciples. To keep building clarity, memorize the discipleship definitions in the back of this workbook and be ready to recite them during your next meeting. Go ahead and practice here:

A disciple is a person who is _____

_____ .

Disciple making is Jesus' intentional process of _____

_____

_____ .

Pray: A.C.T.S.

11

MARK 4: TEACH

Application Follow-Up: Recite the two discipleship definitions to one another.

Read Mark 4:1-41 out loud with your discipleship group, and your leader will help you answer the observation, interpretation, and application questions.

OBSERVE: What Do You See?

- Take note: _____ percent of Mark 4 is comprised of four parables. A parable is a short story that teaches a spiritual truth. All four parables Jesus shared in Mark 4 are about _____ : scattering, growing, and harvesting it.

- Scan Mark 4 and underline every reference to listening or hearing. How many did you find in the ESV? _____ As followers of Jesus listen to God's Word and accept it, they learn to hear Jesus' voice.

1. What is God's Word? This is important. God's Word is the _____ as a whole (2 Tim. 3:16), the _____ in general (Matt. 7:24), and the _____ in particular (Mark 1:15).

2. When Jesus interpreted the Parable of the Sower from Mark 4:1-12 to his disciples in Mark 4:13-20, what did he say about the seed scattered on each of the four soils?

The Path:

Rocky Ground:

Thorns:

Good Soil:

INTERPRET: What Does It Mean?

3. Which of the four soils in Jesus' parable best describes you right now? Explain.

4. Jesus wants fourth-soil kinds of people and calls us to disciple fourth-soil people, too! The one difference between the fourth-soilers in Jesus' parable and the other three soils was that fourth-soilers hear God's Word and _____ it (Mark 4:20). This results in producing fruit—thirtyfold, sixtyfold, and a hundredfold!

5. What does it mean to *accept* God's Word? Read James 1:22.

APPLY: How Does It Apply?

6. The "Gospel of Mark Reading" Project: As we accept God's Word, we will learn to _____ Jesus' voice (John 10:27). Read through Mark's Gospel as a whole this week. If you read for fifteen minutes each day, you should finish reading it in seven days. As you read, ask God to teach you to accept his Word and hear Jesus' voice.

Pray: A.C.T.S.

MARK 5: SERVE

Application Follow-Up: What was it like to read Mark's entire Gospel last week?

Read Mark 5:1-43 out loud with your discipleship group, and your leader will help you answer the observation, interpretation, and application questions.

OBSERVE: What Do You See?

- Note: Jesus consistently did three things in each chapter of Mark's Gospel so far, including here in Mark 5. He was _____ , _____ , and _____ .

- Jesus set this Disciple-Teach-Serve (D.T.S.) pattern so we would follow it (e.g., John 13:15; 1 Pet. 2:21). Although all three are present in previous chapters, take note of the emphasis on *discipling* in Mark 3, *teaching* in Mark 4, and *serving* here in Mark 5.

Historical Insight on "Clean and Unclean": Jesus' twelve disciples were Jewish men, which meant they tried to live according to the Old Testament Law. The Law classified many things as either "clean" or "unclean." If a Jew came into contact with something unclean, they had to go through a very involved "cleansing" process. Jesus' disciples had lived their whole lives avoiding "unclean" things, but in Mark 5, Jesus led them into a lot of "uncleanness"!

1. What is the common phrase in Mark 4:35, 5:1, and 5:21 used to describe the place Jesus took his disciples?

2. Mark describes five "unclean" things in verses 1-20. What are they?

-

-

-

-

-

3. Knowing Jewish people tried to avoid everything "unclean," how do you think the disciples felt about Jesus serving this unclean man on the other side?

INTERPRET: What Does It Mean?

4. Jesus' ultimate goal was to train his twelve disciples to "_____ into *all the world* and proclaim the gospel" and to "_____, make disciples of *all nations*" (Mark 6:15; Matt. 28:19). When Jesus took The Twelve to "the other side" in Mark 5, he was training them to _____. A critical aspect of following Jesus—learning to live with Jesus and love others like Jesus—is learning to _____ serve people with the gospel on "the other side."

APPLY: How Does It Apply?

Where is "the other side" in your community? Where are the sick, lonely, poor, or homeless people you can serve? Write down three places.

"The Other Side" Project: When we read of Jesus doing something with his disciples, we should seek to put it into practice (cf. 1 John 2:6). Jesus took his disciples to "the other side" as part of teaching them to follow him, so *go* with your discipleship group this week to "the other side" and serve people in need with the gospel. Agree on a service project and do it together. There are some thought-provoking ideas in the "40 Ways to Serve" list (available for download at www.himpublications.com/downloads). Go together to serve, not alone.

Pray: A.C.T.S.

MARK 6: SERVANT-LEADERSHIP

Application Follow-Up: What did you learn by going to "the other side"?

Read Mark 6:1-56 out loud with your discipleship group, and your leader will help you answer the observation, interpretation, and application questions.

OBSERVE: What Do You See?

- Jesus' "D.T.S." pattern continues in Mark 6. We see him continue *Discipling* (verse _____), *Teaching* (verse _____), and *Serving* people (verse _____). Keep looking for this pattern as you read each chapter of Mark.
- In Mark 6, Jesus sent out his disciples two by two to do what he had been doing. This was the first time he had sent them out like this so that they could labor *with him*. It was a step up in their servant-leadership training.

1. Carefully read Mark 6:7-13. What instructions did Jesus give The Twelve as he sent them out? In verse 11, what did Jesus anticipate they would encounter?

2. Mark 6:12-13 makes it clear that the disciples went out and did what Jesus had been doing. How was this "taking it to the next level" for the disciples?

INTERPRET: What Does It Mean?

3. What happened in Mark 6:7-13 was a major discipleship moment, a new stage of Jesus' servant-leadership training. This was the third of four stages in his training:

- _____ at Jesus ("Come and see" from John 1:46).

- _____ from Jesus ("Come, be with me" from Mark 3:14).

- _____ with Jesus ("Go, do as I do" from Mark 6:7).

- _____ for Jesus ("Go, make disciples" from Matt. 28:19).

16

4. In Mark 6, the disciples saw Jesus _____ in Nazareth (6:3), Jesus instructed them on what to do when they faced _____ (6:11), and John the Baptist was _____ (6:27). As you grow in servant-leadership, you should expect increasing levels of opposition, suffering, and even persecution.

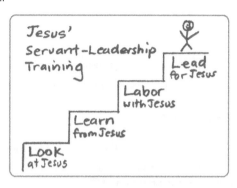

5. As Jesus continued training his disciples, it became clear that there's a cost to following Jesus. Read John 15:18-21. What questions does this raise for you?

APPLY: How Does It Apply?

As you consider the four stages of Jesus' servant-leadership training, which stage are you in right now? Explain why you see yourself in that stage.

The "Persecution Research" Project: Visit a website about Christian persecution (e.g., www.opendoorsusa.org) and spend ten minutes learning about Christian persecution in the world today. Write down what you learn and any other thoughts about persecution below.

Pray: A.C.T.S.

MARK 7: HARD-HEARTEDNESS

Application Follow-Up: What were your impressions of Christian persecution from www.opendoorsusa.org or a similar website?

Read Mark 7:1-37 out loud with your discipleship group, and your leader will help you answer the observation, interpretation, and application questions.

OBSERVE: What Do You See?

- The first half of Mark 7 dealt with Jewish traditions of washing and ways of honoring parents. Learn about these things, but don't be distracted from the main warning against having a hard heart.

- Be sure to take note that Jesus specifically talked with his disciples about "the heart" at two poignant moments in Mark 7: first in verse _____ and then again in verse _____ .

1. We're studying Mark 7, but look back at Mark 6:52. Does it surprise you that after his disciples spent time being with Jesus, they still had hard hearts?

2. How many "evils" did Jesus name in Mark 7:21-22? _____ . Write each of the "evils" Jesus named:

3. What did Jesus teach us about the heart in verses 1-23? How would you summarize his teaching so that you could explain it to someone else?

INTERPRET: What Does It Mean?

4. Following Jesus involves being acutely aware of our own hard-heartedness. Jesus taught us that out of our heart come all kinds of _____ (a.k.a. _____). Sin is anything we _____ , _____ , or _____ that is against God's Law.

5. What did Jesus mean when he spoke of "the heart"? Write a simple definition for it here. The heart is . . .

6. Evil thoughts come out of our heart and inform our mind. What did Paul say in Romans 12:2 must happen with the mind of a follower of Jesus?

7. Read Psalm 32, Ezekiel 36:25-26, and 1 John 1:8-10. How do these passages say our sins can be forgiven and we can receive a new heart?

APPLY: How Does It Apply?

The Five-Day "Evil Thought Journal" Project: Identify one evil thought that came out of your heart each day for five days and circle a word or write a new word around the heart drawing (above) for each thought. Then, humble yourself before God and confess each evil thought to him in prayer. Allow the truths from Psalm 32, Ezekiel 36, and 1 John 1 to fill your mind.

Pray: A.C.T.S.

MARK 8: GOSPEL FULLNESS

Application Follow-Up: What did you learn from the "Evil Thought Journal"?

Read Mark 8:1-38 out loud with your discipleship group, and your leader will help answer the observation, interpretation, and application questions.

OBSERVE: What Do You See?

- Mark 8 is a very important chapter. It's not only the halfway point of Mark's Gospel, but it's also the turning point. Jesus brings all the essential elements of *the gospel of the kingdom of God* together in Mark 8.

- Until this point in Mark's Gospel, many people have said many things about whom they thought Jesus was. Surprisingly, The Twelve said nothing except asking, "Who is this?" (Mark 4:41)!

1. Read Mark 8:27-31. What question did Jesus very pointedly ask The Twelve in verse 29? How did Peter answer?

2. Historical Insight on "Christ": Christ means "_____ ," which carries the idea of God's Anointed King. "Christ" is not a name; it's a _____ given to *the One about whom all Scripture is written* and *the One who fulfills all Scripture*, including fulfilling more than _____ Old Testament prophecies. To say Jesus is "the Christ" is to acknowledge he is God in the flesh, God's Anointed King, God's one and only Son, the Savior of the World.

3. After Peter's confession, what did Jesus begin teaching The Twelve in Mark 8:31? Be specific. (This was the first time Jesus spoke of these things; see also Mark 9:30-32 and 10:32-34—three times in three chapters!)

INTERPRET: What Does It Mean?

4. In Mark 1:14-17, we learned of four essential elements of Jesus' gospel. In Mark 8:27-31, we learn three more. With your leader's help, list all seven.

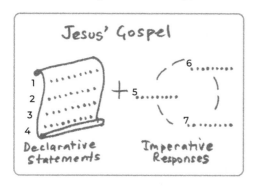

5. Read about the gospel in 1 Corinthians 15:1-5. What similarities do you notice about what Paul writes there and what Jesus tells his disciples in Mark 8:27-31?

APPLY: How Does It Apply?

At this point in your journey with Jesus, if Jesus asked you, "Who do you say I am?" what would you say?

The "Gospel Memorization" Project: Read the 101-word gospel definition of "The Discipleship Gospel" at the end of this workbook. Read it each day for five days. Try to memorize it this week and recite to your discipleship group at your next meeting.

Pray: A.C.T.S.

HALFWAY CHECK-IN POINT

Congratulations! Now that you've completed the first eight chapters of Mark, you're halfway through the workbook.

Leaders, remember from the Leader's Guide at the beginning of the workbook that the halfway point is when you start letting group members take turns leading the group. Schedule each member of the group to lead one or two chapters from here on out. Jesus delegated responsibility to help his disciples grow, so learn from him by delegating. Ask God to help you train each member to become a disciple-making leader.

After the Mark 12 study, the application project includes reading a very short book called *The False Promise of Discipleship*. This is available as a free eBook from www.himpublications.com/downloads, but if your group prefers reading the print version, go ahead and order print copies now so they can arrive before your group meets to study Mark 12 in a few weeks.

Group members, take heart and keep going—you're halfway there! Those who finish this study gain crystal clarity on the meaning of the gospel, what discipleship means for them, and how to make disciples. In other words, finishing helps equip you for participating in Jesus' Great Commission (Matt. 28:18-20).

What has been the best thing about your experience with this training so far?

How has God been good to you? For what can you give God praise?

We recommend the following supplemental readings from *The Discipleship Gospel** as you continue this discipleship experience through the Gospel of Mark:

- Read Chapters 1-3 in *The Discipleship Gospel* for an introduction to the seven elements of the gospel and a detailed explanation of why understanding the gospel is so critical.
- Read Chapters 4-9 in *The Discipleship Gospel* to go deeper into the meaning of each of the seven elements of the gospel and an explanation of our 101-word definition of the gospel.

*Purchase this resource at www.himpublications.com.

MARK 9: THE KINGDOM OF GOD

Application Follow-Up: Recite the 101-word definition of the gospel.

Read Mark 9:1-50 out loud with your discipleship group and answer the observation, interpretation, and application questions.

OBSERVE: What Do You See?

- The phrase "the kingdom of God" appears in Mark 9:1 and 9:47. These two references, at the beginning and at the end of Mark 9, help us understand that this whole chapter is about God's kingdom.

- Definition: The kingdom of God is _____ over all things in heaven and on earth through Jesus of Nazareth, who is the Christ.

1. What did Jesus say in Mark 9:1 some of his disciples would see?

2. Write down four ways Peter, James, and John experienced "the kingdom of God" *with power* on the mountain in Mark 9:2-13:

-

-

-

-

3. Read 2 Peter 1:16-18. These verses record the Apostle Peter's account of Jesus' transfiguration on the mountain. What did you learn from reading them?

INTERPRET: What Does It Mean?

4. In Mark 9, we see that Jesus revealed God's kingdom with power. Being a follower of Jesus means you accept the truth that _____ and believe in the reality of _____ . When you consider how God's kingdom has already come, it's helpful to know this: wherever Christ _____ , there is God's kingdom.

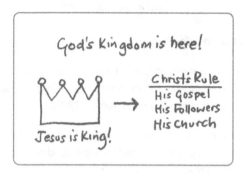

5. Other Kingdom Teachings: Here are three more truths Jesus taught about his kingdom:

- Many of Jesus' parables were about what the kingdom of God is like, including the Parable of _____ (Mark 4:30-32), which teaches that God's kingdom starts small and grows big.
- Jesus taught that God's kingdom has _____ come but is _____ here in all its fullness (Luke 17:20-21; Matt. 25:31-46).
- Jesus said his kingdom was _____ (John 18:36).

APPLY: How Does It Apply?

6. Jesus taught us to pray for God's kingdom to come on earth as it is in heaven (Matt. 6:9-13). When you pray for God's kingdom to come, you are:

- Expressing your faith in Jesus as _____
- Inviting Jesus to _____ your life
- Praying for God's eternal kingdom to _____
- Committing to _____ the gospel of the kingdom now

The "Lord's Prayer" Project: Use the Lord's Prayer (Matt. 6:9-13) notecard at the back of this workbook to memorize Jesus' prayer before your next meeting.

Pray: A.C.T.S.

MARK 10: RENOUNCEMENT

Application Follow-Up: What did you learn as you prayed the Lord's Prayer?

Read Mark 10:1-52 out loud with your discipleship group and answer the observation, interpretation, and application questions.

OBSERVE: What Do You See?

- In Mark 10, we see Jesus discipling, teaching, and serving in the face of opposition, as we've already seen him doing. One thing that stands out in Mark 10 is his interaction with the rich man (vv. 17-31).

- Take note of the phrases "inherit eternal life" (v. 17), "enter the kingdom of God" (v. 23), and "be saved" (v. 26)—that they are used synonymously during Jesus' interaction with the rich man.

1. In Mark 10:17, the rich man asked Jesus what he needed to do to inherit eternal life. What did he tell the man to do in verse 21?

2. Did Jesus' answer surprise you in any way?

3. How did the rich man respond to Jesus' call in verse 22?

INTERPRET: What Does It Mean?

4. The burning question is this: does Jesus call *everyone to sell all their earthly possessions* to inherit eternal life? The answer is _____ . He may call some to do it, though—like the rich man in Mark 10! Is Christ calling you to sell everything you have and give it to the poor so you can follow him?

5. Read Luke 14:33. While Jesus doesn't call all his followers to sell everything they have, he did call all his followers to "renounce" (ESV) everything they have. What does it mean to "renounce" something?

6. Read Mark 10:28-31. How would Jesus' words in these verses have reassured Peter and the other disciples? How are they challenging to you?

Remember from Mark 4:18-20 that "the deceitfulness of riches" chokes God's Word in our lives and stops us from following Jesus.

"He is no fool who gives what he cannot keep to gain what he cannot lose." —Jim Elliott

7. Read Matthew 6:19-21. How does Jesus' teaching on treasures and the heart add to your understanding of renouncement?

APPLY: How Does It Apply?

The **"Renouncement Prayer" Project:** Pray a prayer of renouncement once a day for five days. Find a quiet place and pray, *"Lord, I want to make you most important in my life. Is there anything I consider more important than you? Is there anything I am not willing to give up for you?"* After asking this of the Lord in prayer, sit quietly and listen for him. If something comes to mind, write it down and consider whether or not you need to renounce it before the Lord.

Pray: A.C.T.S.

MARK 11: FORGIVING OTHERS

Application Follow-Up: Did the Lord speak to you about renouncing anything?

Read Mark 11:1-33 out loud with your discipleship group and answer the observation, interpretation, and application questions.

OBSERVE: What Do You See?

- Mark 11 marks the beginning of the last week of Jesus' life. The first two-thirds of Mark's Gospel covered three years. The last one-third—Mark 11-16—spans just one week. This indicates the importance of the last week!

- Mark 11 also contains Jesus' first teaching in Mark's Gospel on prayer. It's worth noting that his teaching on prayer here has to do with
_____ .

1. What does Jesus call the Temple in Mark 11:17? (Clue: He calls it three things.)

-

-

-

2. While Jesus was on his way to the Temple, which was "a house of prayer," what did he teach his disciples about prayer in Mark 11:25?

INTERPRET: What Does It Mean?

If we have *anything* against *anyone*, Jesus calls us to pray. We should pray that God will change our heart and enable us (by his Holy Spirit) to truly forgive them. As followers of Jesus, we need to put Jesus' teaching in Mark 11:25 into practice.

3. Mark 11:25 is just one of a handful of verses *strongly* connecting God's forgiveness of our sins with our forgiveness of others' sins. Read the following verses and summarize what they teach us about this connection:

Matthew 6:14-15:

Ephesians 4:32:

Colossians 3:12-14:

"Everyone thinks forgiveness is a lovely idea until he has something to forgive." — C.S. Lewis

4. Read Matthew 18:21-35. We must be willing to forgive others from our heart. How is Jesus' teaching in Mark 11:25 consistent with Matthew 18:21-35?

APPLY: How Does It Apply?

The "Forgiveness Prayer" Project: Pray the Lord's Prayer in Matthew 6:9-13—the same prayer we prayed when we studied Mark 9 (above)—each day for five days. This prayer includes asking God to forgive you in the same way you have forgiven others. If God brings someone to mind you have not forgiven as you pray, put Jesus' words from Mark 11:25 into practice and pray until God softens your heart to truly forgive them.

Pray: A.C.T.S.

MARK 12: LOVING OTHERS

Application Follow-Up: Whom did the Lord bring to your mind to forgive?

Read Mark 12:1-44 out loud with your discipleship group and answer the observation, interpretation, and application questions.

OBSERVE: What Do You See?

- Jesus was asked one of the most controversial questions of his time in Mark 12: Which of the _____ commandments in the Old Testament is the most important?

- Jesus' answer had to do with loving others. This helps us understand that the basic orientation of our lives as followers of Jesus is to be _____ , not self-centered.

1. According to Jesus, what are the *two* most important commandments in the Old Testament? How would you summarize them?

- _____ (Deut. 6:4-5)

- _____ (Lev. 19:18)

2. Now that you've read these verses, what about Jesus' answer stands out to you?

INTERPRET: What Does It Mean?

3. Read John 13:34-35. Jesus' teaching about a new commandment is similar to *and different from* his most important commandment teaching. How are they similar? How are they different?

4. As we consider how to love others just as Jesus has loved us, we need to know two things. First, we are commanded to _____ ,

which is to say with his kind of love. Second, the only way we can do this is by being filled with his love, which begins when we _____

_____ .

5. Read 1 John 4:19-21. What do these verses teach us about the connection between our love for God and loving others?

APPLY: How Does It Apply?

The "Jesus Paradigm" Project: Go to www.himpublications.com/downloads to download a free eBook called *The False Promise of Discipleship*. (You may also order print copies from there.) This very short book will help you to think about God's love through the "Jesus Paradigm." After you read it, complete the section below.

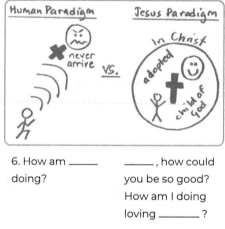

6. How am _____   _____ , how could
doing?   you be so good?
                       How am I doing
                       loving _____ ?

7. Read Ephesians 1:3-14 and note how this passage reinforces the Jesus Paradigm. What ten things do these verses teach us God has done for us "in Christ"?

-
-
-
-
-

    -
    -
    -
    -
    -

Pray: A.C.T.S.

MARK 13: THE SECOND COMING

Application Follow-Up: Talk about the "Jesus Paradigm Project."

Read Mark 13:1-37 out loud with your discipleship group. What are the three aspects of Bible study?

1. _____ 2. _____ 3. _____

OBSERVE: What Do You See?

- As we've noted in previous chapters, Mark 11-16 records the events of the final week before Jesus' crucifixion. Mark 13 happened the Tuesday night before his crucifixion, which happened on a Friday.

- Mark 13 contains one of Jesus' greatest prophecies: his prophecy regarding the destruction of the _____ in Jerusalem! This prophecy is also connected to the promise of his _____ .

1. Read Mark 13:1-2 carefully. What "great buildings" was Jesus referring to in verse 2? What did Jesus say would happen to these great buildings?

2. In response to this prophecy, what questions did his disciples ask in verse 4?

When...

What...

3. In Mark 13:30, Jesus answered his disciples' first question about *when* the Temple would be destroyed. When did he say it would be destroyed?

4. There are many signs in Mark 13, but one stands out: the sign in verse 14, which answers the disciples' second question. One characteristic that makes the sign in verse 14 stand out is Mark's editorial words, "Let the reader

understand...." Such a note is rare and should catch our attention as readers. What was the sign in Mark 13:14?

INTERPRET: What Does It Mean?

5. Jesus' great prophecy about the destruction of the Temple within a generation was fulfilled in _____ . The Roman army, led by the future Emperor Titus, utterly destroyed the Temple, and thus, Jesus' prophecy in Mark 13 was fulfilled exactly as he predicted.

6. The fulfillment of Jesus' great prophecy about the Temple's destruction should give us great confidence in his promise regarding his _____ (Mark 13:26-27). Followers of Jesus believe he is coming again to establish God's eternal kingdom, just as he said.

APPLY: How Does It Apply?

Do you believe Christ is coming again to establish God's eternal kingdom?

The "Prophecy Study" Project: Using the Bible-study skills you've been learning, study Jesus' prophecy in Matthew 25:31-46. Write down your notes as you practice your observation, interpretation, and application skills. As you apply this passage, answer this question: How should believing in Jesus' second coming change the way you live now? You can access a brief study guide for this project at www.himpublications.com/downloads. Bring your study notes to your next discipleship-group meeting.

Pray: A.C.T.S.

MARK 14: THE LORD'S SUPPER

Application Follow-Up: Share what you learned from Matthew 25:31-46.

Read Mark 14:1-72 out loud with your discipleship group and answer the observation, interpretation, and application questions.

OBSERVE: What Do You See?

- Mark 14:1 says it was "two days before the Passover," which meant it was the Wednesday before that Good Friday when Jesus was crucified. For this reason, every thing we read in Mark 14 comes with a certain kind of intensity.

- A lot happened in Mark 14: Judas betrays Jesus, Jesus prays and is arrested, the disciples desert Jesus. The quietest, and maybe most enduring, moment was Jesus' "last supper" with his disciples.

1. Carefully reread Mark 14:22-25. Write down *everything* Jesus did in these verses. (Clue: He did 10 things.)

-                                •
-                                •
-                                •
-                                •
-                                •

2. What did Jesus say in these verses about the bread and the cup?

INTERPRET: What Does It Mean?

3. To supplement Mark 14:22-25, read the instructions the Apostle Paul received from Jesus about the "Lord's Supper" in 1 Corinthians 11:23-32. The "Lord's

Supper" is eating the bread and drinking the cup with the church (1 Cor. 11:20). This sacred meal is also called "Holy Communion" or the "Eucharist." After reading the Apostle Paul's instructions in 1 Corinthians 11, list three reasons we continue to share the Lord's Supper on a regular basis as followers of Jesus?

-

-

-

4. As followers of Jesus, we are to obey his instructions about the Lord's Supper. We should regularly share the Lord's Supper with other followers of Jesus. As we do, we _____ him, _____ ourselves, _____ we're living in the blessings of the new covenant, and _____ that sharing "proclaims the Lord's death until he comes."

APPLY: How Does It Apply?

The "Bread and Cup" Project: Jesus shared the "Last Supper" with his disciples in Mark 14. Gather together for a meal with your discipleship group just like you did after the Mark 2 study. This time, after the meal, share the bread and cup of the Lord's Supper together. Your discipleship group leader can lead that time by reading 1 Corinthians 11:23-32, breaking the bread, and sharing the cup with the group. As you share the Lord's Supper, do it in remembrance of Jesus.
Note: The Lord's Supper is intended only for those who have committed their lives to following Jesus, which begins by repenting of sin and believing in the gospel. Have you committed your life to following Jesus?

Pray: A.C.T.S.

MARK 15: JESUS' DEATH

Application Follow-Up: What were your impressions of the Lord's Supper?

Read Mark 15:1-47 out loud with your discipleship group and answer the observation, interpretation, and application questions.

OBSERVE: What Do You See?

- Everything in Mark's Gospel from Mark 8:31 until this point had looming over it the dark shadow of Jesus' impending death. This gives Mark 15, which records Jesus' death, a very climactic feel to it.

- There's nothing more important to being a follower of Jesus than believing in his death and resurrection. With regard to his death, we're called to believe Jesus died _____ .

1. Mark 15:37-39 records the last moments of Jesus' death. What words did Mark use to communicate his death?

2. What happens in Mark 15:39-47 that confirms Jesus' death?

INTERPRET: What Does It Mean?

3. What do you learn from the following three verses about Jesus' death?

Romans 5:8:

1 Corinthians 15:3:

1 Peter 3:18:

4. How do the three verses above make Jesus' death personal to you?

5. To truly begin following Jesus, we must believe Jesus died _____ .
Jesus' death also helps us grasp the meaning of his words in Mark 8:34, where
he called his followers to _____ (Luke 9:23 includes the
word "daily").

"People who are truly following Jesus have a faith
in Christ's death that leads them to crucify
their flesh [daily]." —The Discipleship Gospel

6. What do the passages below teach about daily crucifying our sin?

Romans 6:10-11:

Romans 8:13:

Galatians 5:24:

APPLY: How Does It Apply?

The "Take Up Your Cross" Project: Memorize Luke 9:23 using the notecard in
the back of this workbook. Do you believe in your heart that Jesus is the Christ
and that he died on the cross for your sins? Are you willing to *deny yourself, take
up your cross daily,* and *follow Christ,* even if it means suffering for his sake (see
Mark 6 study)? Carefully consider these questions, count the cost, and talk with
your discipleship group leader about Christ's death.

Pray: A.C.T.S.

MARK 16: JESUS' RESURRECTION

Application Follow-Up: Do you truly believe in your heart that Jesus died for your sins? Are you committed to taking up your cross daily to follow Jesus?

Read Mark 16:1-20 out loud with your discipleship group and answer the observation, interpretation, and application questions.

OBSERVE: What do you see?

- Jesus made his entire ministry dependent on one miraculous sign: his _____ (Matt. 12:39-40). This miraculous sign alone proves Jesus is the Christ, God's _____ .

- Jesus' resurrection has more supporting evidence than almost any event in ancient history. One introductory resource for the evidence for Jesus' resurrection is Lee Strobel's book *The Case for Christ*.

1. How does Mark 16 describe the circumstances when the women discovered Jesus had been raised from the dead?

2. Read Mark 8:31, 9:31, and 10:34. Jesus told his disciples about his resurrection before he was raised from the dead. Why do you think he did this?

3. What did Jesus say to his disciples after his resurrection (vv. 14-16)?

INTERPRET: What Does It Mean?

4. Read Romans 10:9. What does this verse teach us about conversion?

5. If you are going to follow Christ, it is crucial to understand the Apostle Paul's teaching that *the same power that raised Christ from the dead lives in you* and _____ . What do the following verses teach you about the power of Jesus' resurrection dwelling in us?

Romans 6:1-11:

Romans 8:9-11:

Ephesians 1:16-20:

6. Read Romans 6:3-11. In what ways does being baptized in water enact our faith in the gospel as we commit ourselves to new life in Jesus?

APPLY: How Does It Apply?

Believe and Be Baptized: If you believe in the gospel, which climaxes with Jesus' resurrection, you will obey Jesus' command to be baptized (Mark 16:16). If you are ready to commit your life to following Jesus with no conditions and no excuses, talk to your discipleship group leader about being baptized. Remember, the Holy Spirit will empower you to follow in Jesus' footsteps, including being baptized like Jesus (Mark 1:9-11).

Note: Many early manuscripts do not include Mark 16:9-20, but we have included it here to honor the translations and traditions that include it.

Pray: A.C.T.S.

AFTER YOU'VE BEEN BAPTIZED, WHAT'S NEXT?

If you have begun following Jesus and been baptized, consider taking these next steps:

Read *The Discipleship Gospel*

The Discipleship Gospel goes deeper into the ideas of this workbook. As we mentioned at the halfway point, Chapters 1-9 introduce and describe the seven elements of the gospel. Once you've read those chapters, pick up with Chapter 10 and read through the end to learn more about how to be a disciple and make disciples in the life-giving community of a local church.

Join a Gospel-Preaching Church

The church is critical to Jesus' plan for advancing the gospel of the kingdom throughout the world. If you aren't a member of a gospel-preaching church, join one in your area as soon as possible (1 Cor. 12:12-13; Heb. 10:25, Philem. 6). Your unity with others who worship and love Jesus will spur you on to serve his kingdom-advancing purposes in the world. Talk to your discipleship group leader about joining their church as a member.

Lead a Discipleship Group

It's one thing to be *led* through this discipleship experience; it's a very different thing to *lead* a discipleship group yourself. It requires you to rely upon the Holy Spirit! You complete your discipleship training in "the elementary doctrine of Christ" and the basic commands of Jesus when you have not only been discipled but have also made disciples (Matt. 28:19). Talk to your discipleship group leader about what's involved in leading a group and whether or not you are ready to lead (or be an apprentice leader).

Discover Your Spiritual Gifts

The Holy Spirit dwells in all followers of Jesus, but he also uniquely gives "spiritual gifts" to each individual follower of Jesus (Rom. 12:1-8; 1 Cor. 12:1-31, Eph. 4:1-16). To begin discovering your spiritual gifts, you might want to take a free online "spiritual gifts survey" by visiting gifts.churchgrowth.org (or another reliable assessment provider). After that, talk with your discipleship group leader about the results and how your gifts might be uniquely matched with a kingdom-advancing ministry of your local church.

ANSWER KEY

As You Go Through This Workbook

Take advantage of these helpful, supplemental resources that we've selected specifically for this workbook. They will help you go deeper into this study, in addition to reading *The Discipleship Gospel* to which this workbook is a companion:

- N.T. Wright's *Mark for Everyone* (Louisville: Westminster John Knox Press, 2004): A helpful and accessible commentary on Mark's Gospel.
- Howard Hendricks's *Living By The Book* (Chicago: Moody Press, 1991): A guide for learning how to study Scripture.
- Bill Hull's *Conversion and Discipleship: You Can't Have One Without the Other* (Grand Rapids: Zondervan, 2016): A description of the most common false gospels today.
- John Walvoord and Roy Zuck's *The Bible Knowledge Commentary* (1983), and I. Howard Marshal and A.R. Millard's *New Bible Dictionary* (1996): A Bible commentary and a dictionary for learning to study God's Word.

MARK 1: OBSERVE: thirty / gospel, gospel. 1) Jesus declared, "The time is fulfilled and the kingdom of God is at hand." 2) Repent of sin, believe in the gospel, follow me. 3) follow me. 4) Kingdom, Repent, Believe, Follow. **INTERPRET:** 5) Rom. 1:16: The gospel is the power of God for the salvation of everyone who believes; 1 Cor. 15:1-3: The gospel is of first importance.

Mark 2: OBSERVE: the Christ. 1) Mark 2:7: *Who can forgive sins but God alone*? Jesus had the authority to forgive sins. 2) Mark 2:16: *Why does Jesus eat with sinners*? Jesus implied he has the power to justify sinners (to declare them righteous before God). 3) Mark 2:18: *Why weren't Jesus' disciples fasting*? Three / Jesus implies he's the Bridegroom, which fulfills Isa. 61:10. 4) Mark 2:24: *Why didn't Jesus' disciples observe Sabbath rules?* / David / the son of David (see also Mark 10:47). **INTERPRET:** 5) Jesus claimed to be the Christ—the Bridegroom and the son of David of the Old Testament—with the power to forgive sins and the authority to justify sinners.

MARK 3: OBSERVE: 1) First: To be with Jesus. 2) Second: To preach the gospel; Third: To cast out demons with authority (and heal the sick, Matt. 10:1). **INTERPRET:** 3) twelve / three. 4) The religious leaders recognized that Peter and John had been with Jesus. 5) Jesus is at the center of any discipleship group: We read about him, talk about him, learn his teaching, put his teaching into practice, pray in his name, and he promises his presence is with us (Matt. 28:18-20). **APPLY:** A disciple is a person who is... learning to live with Jesus and love others like Jesus / Disciple making is Jesus' intentional process of...

servant-leadership training that multiplies disciples a few at a time to build up the church and advance God's kingdom throughout the world.

MARK 4: OBSERVE: 85 / God's Word / Twelve. 1) Bible / teachings of Jesus / gospel. 2) The Path: Satan takes God's Word from some people as soon as they hear it (4:15); Rocky Ground: Some people receive God's Word with joy, but they don't allow it to grow deep roots in their lives and they fall away (4:16-17); Thorns: Some people hear God's Word, but the cares of the world, the deceitfulness of riches, and the desires for other things choke it out (4:18-19); Good Soil: Other people hear God's Word, accept it, and God's Word multiplies in and through their lives with outstanding fruit (4:20). **INTERPRET:** 3) Answers vary. 4) accept. 5) To accept God's Word means you obey it, put it into practice, and do it. **APPLY:** 6) hear.

MARK 5: OBSERVE: discipling / teaching / serving. 1) "The other side." 2) Five *unclean* things: the Gerasenes = Gentiles, thus *unclean* territory (5:1); *unclean* tombs (5:2); *unclean* spirit (5:2); the Gentile, unclean man (5:2); *unclean* pigs (5:11). 3) Maybe confused, angry, or upset. **INTERPRET:** 4. Go / Go / go / go.

MARK 6: OBSERVE: 6:1 / 6:2 / 6:5. 1) Jesus instructed them in what to take and not to take with them and to "shake off the dust that is on your feet as a testimony against them;" He anticipated his disciples would encounter opposition as they went out to do what he had been doing. 2) They were no longer merely *watching* Jesus do the work, but also *doing* his work. **INTERPRET:** 3) *Look* at Jesus / *Learn* from Jesus / *Labor* with Jesus / *Lead* for Jesus. 4) rejected / opposition / beheaded. 5) Answers vary.

MARK 7: OBSERVE: v. 6 / v. 21. 1) Answers vary. 2) Twelve (twelve disciples, twelve sins!): sexual immorality, theft, murder, adultery, coveting, wickedness, deceit, sensuality, envy, slander, pride, and foolishness. 3) Every day sin seeks to harden our heart to God; if we don't humble ourselves before God, our heart will remain hard (and maybe even become harder). 4) evil (a.k.a. sin) / think / say / do. **INTERPRET:** 5) The heart is *that spiritual part of us that without Christ turns against God.* 6) We must be transformed by the renewal of our minds through Scripture and the Holy Spirit. 7) Psalm 32: If we humble ourselves and acknowledge our sin before God in prayer, God promises to forgive our sins / Ezekiel 36:25-26: God is the one who removes our hard heart and gives us a new one / 1 John 1:8-10: Confessing our sins to God elicits forgiveness from God; we can trust in his forgiveness because he is faithful and just.

MARK 8: OBSERVE: 1) Jesus asked, "But who do you say I am?" Peter answered, "You are the Christ!" 2) Anointed One / title / 400. 3) His death ("killed") and his resurrection ("after three days rise again"). **INTERPRET:** 4) Declarative Statements: the *kingdom* of God (1:15), Jesus is the *Christ* (8:29), his *death* (8:31), his *resurrection* (8:31); Imperative Responses: *repent* of sin (1:15), *believe* the gospel (1:15), *follow* Jesus (1:17, 8:34). 5) These passages are strikingly similar, except Paul goes into more detail in 1 Cor. 15 (e.g., Paul states that Jesus died *for our sins,* 15:3).

MARK 9: OBSERVE: God's rule. 1) The kingdom of God coming with power. 2) Jesus was transfigured (9:2) / his clothes were radiant white (9:3) / Elijah's and Moses's appearance (9:4) / a voice said, "This is my beloved Son" (9:7). 3) In 2 Peter 1, the Apostle Peter wrote that Jesus' transfiguration was powerful, that he witnessed Jesus' "majesty," and that God the Father had glorified Jesus. **INTERPRET:** 4) Jesus is God's king / God's kingdom / rules. 5) the Mustard Seed / already come but is not yet / not of this world. APPLY: 5) king, rule, come, declare.

MARK 10: OBSERVE: 1) Jesus told the rich man to sell all he had, give it to the poor, and follow him. 2) It might have surprised some people that Jesus told this man *to do* something to inherit eternal life, not simply to *believe.* 3) The rich man walked away from Jesus disheartened and sorrowful. **INTERPRET:** 4) no / Answers vary. 5) To renounce something means to formally abandon your ownership of it; if you've renounced something to God, you may be in possession of it, but you no longer own it—God does. 6) Mark 10:28-31 would have reassured Peter because he had "left everything" / Answers vary. 7) If our hearts are focused on gaining more earthly treasures, we can't be focused on eternal kingdom treasures, too.

MARK 11: OBSERVE: forgiving others. 1) Jesus calls it "my house," "a house of prayer for all nations," and a "den of robbers." 2) To forgive "anything against anyone" in prayer, so God the Father may forgive them! **INTERPRET:** 3) Matt. 6:14-15: *If* you forgive others, then God will forgive you / Eph. 4:32: Forgive one another *as* (or "in the same way") God in Christ forgave you / Col. 3:12-14: As the Lord has forgiven you, you *must* also forgive. 4) Both Mark 11:25 and Matthew 18:21-35 emphasize the vital importance for followers of Jesus to forgive others.

MARK 12: OBSERVE: 613 / others-focused. 1) Love God / Love others. 2) Answers vary. **INTERPRET:** 3) Similar: Both Jesus' most important commandment and his new commandment are others-focused and love-centered / Different: His new commandment is more specific: not just God but also Jesus, not just neighbors but also one another. 4) love others with Jesus' love / accept Jesus' love for ourselves. 5) 1 John 4:19-21 teaches us that one cannot truly say they love God if they hate another person. **APPLY:** 6) How am *I* doing? / *God,* how can you be so good? / How am I doing loving *others*? 7) This passage reinforces the Jesus Paradigm by teaching that by faith in Christ we are truly "in Christ"—in God's kingdom. / Ephesians 1:3-14 teaches us that God has done at least ten things for us: blessed us (1:3); chosen us (1:4); loved us (1:4); predestined us (1:5); adopted us (1:5); redeemed us (1:7); forgiven us (1:7); knows us (1:9); sealed us by the Holy Spirit (1:13); given us an inheritance (1:14).

MARK 13: The three aspects are observation, interpretation, and application. **OBSERVE:** Temple, second coming. 1) The buildings of the Temple / They would be destroyed. 2) *When* will these things be? / *What* will be the sign these things are about to be accomplished? 3) Within "this generation." 4) The abomination of desolation. **INTERPRET:** 5) 70 A.D. 6) second coming.

MARK 14: OBSERVE: 1) He ate with his disciples, took bread, blessed the bread, broke the bread, gave his disciples bread, said, "Take, this is my body," took a cup, gave thanks, gave the cup to his disciples, said, "This is my blood of the covenant which is poured out for many." 2) The bread is my body; the cup is my blood. **INTERPRET:** 3) Jesus commanded us to / It helps us remember that Christ died for our sins / It proclaims "the Lord's death until he comes." 4) remember / examine / recognize / know.

MARK 15: OBSERVE: for our sins. 1) "breathed his last" (15:37, 39). 2) A centurion witnessed his last breath; women witnessed Jesus' death; the Roman governor, Pilate, confirmed Jesus' death; and Jesus was buried. **INTERPRET:** 3) Rom. 5:8: God showed his love *for us* through Jesus' death / 1 Cor. 15:3: Christ died *for our sins* in accordance with the Scriptures, and the truth of the gospel is of first importance / 1 Pet. 3:18: Christ died *to bring us to God*. 4) Answers vary. 5) for our sins / take up their cross. 6) Rom. 6:10-11: Because of his death, we must consider ourselves dead to sin / Rom. 8:13: If we live by the Holy Spirit, we will put to death the deeds of the flesh / Gal. 5:24: If we belong to Christ, we will crucify our flesh with its sinful desires.

MARK 16: OBSERVE: resurrection / Anointed King. 1) The women saw the very large stone rolled back; they saw a man dressed in white (i.e., an angel, see Matt. 28:2-3); and they heard him say, "He has risen." 2) Answers vary, but perhaps Jesus wanted his disciples to know that his resurrection was always part of God's plan. 3) "Go into all the world and proclaim the gospel, and whoever believes and is baptized will be saved." **INTERPRET:** 4) It teaches us that a person must believe in Jesus' resurrection to be saved. 5) empowers you to obey Christ / Rom. 6:1-11: True followers have been united with Christ in his resurrection and should could count themselves alive to God / Rom. 8:9-11: The Holy Spirit raised Christ from the dead and dwells in all true followers, empowering righteousness in them / Eph. 1:16-20: We can know by experience the same immeasurably great power that raised Christ from the dead. 6) As we go down into the waters of baptism, we enact our faith in Christ's death and commit to dying to ourselves / when we come up out of the water, we enact our faith in Christ's resurrection and commit ourselves to living a new life of following Jesus.

SHARE YOUR JESUS STORY

The questions below offer a practical way to organize your thoughts as you learn how to share the gospel with others (Mark 16:15). It includes the personal impact Jesus has made on your life, as well as the message of the gospel itself. Below or on a separate sheet, write your basic story outline and use it to share your "Jesus Story." Practice with your discipleship group by taking just three to five minutes total. (Note: New believers might consider sharing this at their baptism.)

When you were "lost": Describe what your life was like before you believed in Jesus, including the events in your life that helped you realize you needed Jesus.

When you were "found": Describe what happened when you believed in the gospel and began following Jesus without conditions or excuses. Include here an explanation of the gospel itself with all seven elements.

What Jesus is doing in your life now: Describe how your life has changed since you began truly following Jesus. Include what he has been teaching you recently.

The Discipleship Gospel

The gospel is this: the *Kingdom of God* has come through Jesus of Nazareth. He is *Christ*, the King, God's one and only Son. He *died* on the cross for our sins, was buried, and was *resurrected* on the third day according to the Scriptures. In his great love and by his amazing grace, God our Father saves everyone who *repents* of their sin, *believes* the gospel, and *follows* Jesus in the power of the Holy Spirit. When King Jesus returns on the last day, the great Day of Judgment, everyone who followed him will enter the eternal kingdom of God.

A Disciple

A disciple is a person who is learning to live with Jesus and love others like Jesus.

The Lord's Prayer

Pray then like this: "Our Father in heaven, hallowed be your name. Your kingdom come, your will be done, on earth as it is in heaven. Give us this day our daily bread, and forgive us our debts, as we also have forgiven our debtors. And lead us not into temptation, but deliver us from evil."

—Matthew 6:9-13 (ESV)

Disciple Making

Disciple making is Jesus' intentional process of servant-leadership training that multiplies disciples a few at a time to build up the church and advance God's kingdom throughout the world.

The Cost of Discipleship

And he said to all, "If anyone would come after me, let him deny himself and take up his cross daily and follow me."

—Luke 9:23 (ESV)

Become a HIM Publications Member for access to excellent discipleship resources and special offers:
Go to www.himpublications.com/join

CPSIA information can be obtained
at www.ICGtesting.com
Printed in the USA
LVHW051156280623
750938LV00032B/648